Paradise Drive

Paradise Drive

Winner of the Press 53 Award for Poetry

Poems

Rebecca Foust

Press 53

Winston-Salem

Press 53, LLC
PO Box 30314
Winston-Salem, NC 27130

First Edition

A TOM LOMBARDO POETRY SELECTION

Cover design by Lorna Stevens & Kevin Morgan Watson

Cover photo, "Paradise Drive," Copyright © 2015
by Suzanne Engelberg,
used by permission of the artist.

Author photo by Jeremy Thornton

Printed on acid-free paper
ISBN 978-1-941209-16-5

for pilgrims everywhere and in every time

Acknowledgments

These poems were published, sometimes in a variant form
or under a different title, as follows:

Able Muse, "Lust, Retrieving Her Car," "Resolve," and
 "Syringes 'R' Us"
Alehouse Press, "Indentured"
Ambush Review, "Paradise Drive," reprinted in *God,
 Seed* (Tebot Bach, 2010)
American Arts Quarterly, "Romance"
Birmingham Poetry Review, "The Master's House"
Blueline, "All Dirt Is Holy"
Catamaran Literary Reader, "The Quest"
Cincinnati Review, "Anastrophe Elegy"
Cortland Review, "Blazon"
Crab Creek Review, "California Dreaming"
DMQ Review, "The Options" and "Couldn't She Just"
Eleventh Muse, "Three-Car Garage"
Gargoyle, "War," "I'll Burn My Books," and "Situation"
Green Hills Literary Lantern, "How to Live, Reprise"
The Hopkins Review, "Contradance"
The Hudson Review, "Bright Juice," "Dirt," "Nuns Fret
 Not," and "Preparation for Pirouette"
JAMA, "Refractory"
The Ledge, "Bourbon Elegy," "Hard to Entertain,"
 "Oops," and "Troth"
The Los Angeles Review, "Courtesy Flush"
Margie, "Archimedes' Lever," and "Greed, Exercising
 Noblesse Oblige"
Mezzo Cammin, "Back from Retreat"
Mudfish, "Gluttony, Having an Antiphony"
Mudlark, "Rebuke" and "Food Not Bombs"
North American Review, "Forgotten Image" and "Prayer
 for My New Daughter"

Notre Dame Review, "Bane Laid on Behalf of the Latest Late Wife," "Ennui," "*Je Est un Autre*," "Mayberry 94957," "Meet Pilgrim," "News du Jour," "The New Eugenics," "The Prime Mover," "Rat Diptych," and "Why *Pilgrim*?"

The Offending Adam, "The Market"

Poetry East, "Another Party, Another Bathroom," "Cocktail Party," "Party On," and "You-Know-Where Again"

Raintown Review, "Death by Dodge Sportsman" and "PRIDE, Bickering with Vanity"

Redactions, "ENVY Envying the Venial Sins"

Sand Hill Review, "If Not, Winter"

Smartish Pace, "SLOTH, Just Wanting to Go for a Sail"

The South Carolina Review, "Despair," "Don't Talk about This," "Live in the Moment," "The Ones Pilgrim Likes Best," "The Truth," and "WRATH, Talking about 'The Change'"

Southern Indiana Review, "Family Grammar" and "the fire is falling"

Southern Poetry Review, "Gone to the Dogs"

Spillway, A Poetry Magazine, "Religion," "Stepford Wives Theme Party," "Twelve-Step Meeting," and "Vernal"

Two Review, "Teleology," reprinted in *Verse Daily* and in *God, Seed* (Tebot Bach, 2010)

Valparaiso Poetry Review, "Elocution" and "On the Wagon," reprinted in the *Marin Poetry Center Anthology*

The section titles are from poems by William Blake.

Contents

O EARTH RETURN

Introduction

As poetry series editor for Press 53, and as judge for the first annual Press 53 Award for Poetry, I had the utmost pleasure of reading and considering all 236 entries. As any judge will tell you, some entries are easy to pass over half-way through the first reading. But our 25 semi-finalists each received three readings, and our 10 finalists received four. The final three, five and six readings, and the book you hold in your hands won the competition in my seventh reading. With each reading, good poetry unveils itself to the reader. Rebecca Foust's *Paradise Drive* won over an excellent set of entries, peeling away its layers of figurations along the way. It's a collection of irony and metaphor, metonymy and synecdoche, with a dose of synesthesia. I hope you will love it as I do.

Paradise Drive is a collection of contemporary sonnets whose narrator leads readers on a moral and spiritual pilgrimage from the roots of debt and despair in a small manufacturing town to the wealth and despair in one of the most precious pieces of real estate in the United States.

Foust's pilgrim recounts the travails of her childhood home in Altoona, Pennsylvania where

> Her father smelled like failure because
> he could not pay the bills . . .
> . . . Dad died
> in IRS hock; Mom's heir was Goodwill.
> (p. 15)

. . .
The family tree felled by blood
smoke and gin.
(p.48)

One end point there was divorce, despair, and suicide by
pills and alcohol. And a valuable lesson learned:

Better yourself. Work hard. Save. Pay the Bills.
(p. 15)

Foust's pilgrim took the lesson seriously. The journey from
the land of her despair wound its way to Marin County, in
the shadow of Mt. Tam, where Foust foreshadows

. . . the sky
[was] a wound, the sky vivid and gashed;
each day bound to the last with dark thread
(p. xvii)

She describes a place where greed and envy, vanity and
gluttony are flaunted among other sins, where facelifts,
Botox, and subpoenas populate the A-list parties, where the
women wear "discrete black wool [coats] lined / with pure
mink," (p. 39) where huge charitable donations justify the
lavish lifestyles of 10,000 square-foot homes.

Yes, our home is the size of the Queen Mary 2
but that's OK because we gave so much
money away. We made . . . 41-point font in the program.
(p. 6)

It's a place where dogs are chauffeured, Rolfed, and
shampooed herbally by owners who seem Glad-wrapped

inside their 1-percenter lives. Foust's pilgrim finds herself awash in the metonymies of the rich:

> Cowed by all those straight white teeth . . .
> (p.5)
> . . .
> the pearls, the chefs in white toques,
> the blue-smocked valets, the limestone walks
> to houses glowing like over-lit cruise boats
> docked under old oaks.
> (p. 13)

As the parties and functions progress ad infinitum, Foust's pilgrim grows emotionally nauseous and spends more and more time hiding from the crowd in the bathroom, reading *The Cantos.* Foust's pilgrim's dreams have become a nightmare.

> . . . her dreams
> —Macy's-parade-balloon-sized dreams—
> now lie, a tangle of downed silk and line,
> waist-deep in bright ruin, she labors to sing
> wondering if wanting is, after all, all
> there is. Somewhere far away, old ice recedes;
> somewhere a new war combusts . . .
> (p.3)

The internal conflict becomes "the fear of falling / in love with it all (p. 33) . . . thinking meanwhile about Darfur / and *God, all that food* (p. 32) . . . Something is knocking. The size of the world." (p. 63) Foust's pilgrim literally and metaphorically comprehends the personal, moral, spiritual costs of this pilgrimage.

And the end point for the Marin crowd seems a metaphor for the childhood home that Foust's pilgrim escaped. The spiritual exhaustion of that rich-Californian lifestyle leads to women divorced for the trophy wife, the loss of entitlement when "Marin Man" and other market-manipulators face Federal regulators, and too many cases of suicide by pills, drowning, or leaping from the Golden Gate Bridge.

Too few contemporary poets take up the challenge of the sonnet. Foust succeeds where others may tremble. Her precise rhythms and seemingly casual rhymes captivated me. Her strong voice laced with irony and subversive humor enlightened me. Her precise diction nailed her stories to my chest, and then her luscious figurations transported my imagination far from her pages. I could taste and smell and hear the presence of a highly skilled poet.

Congratulations to Rebecca Foust, winner of the 2015 Press 53 Award for Poetry!

Tom Lombardo
Press 53 Poetry Series Editor

Paradise Drive

Dusk mud flats mottled silver, mauve, five
shades of taupe. Air barrel-aged in live oak
and madrone. Phoenix Lake's green jewel.
Mule deer and the tufted bobcat. Roses
blooming straight through late fall.
Hawthorn leaves in drift, a child's cheek
flushed with sleep. Purple against orange,
maple and sage. Peonies under palms,
cactus next to the fat pout of pink hybrid tea.
Trout lilies and wild iris. Mt. Tam mantled
each dawn in fog, then naked and lit
from within. Winter sunsets, the sky
a wound, the sky vivid and gashed;
each day bound to the last with dark thread.

THE MARRIAGE OF
HEAVEN AND HELL

Meet Pilgrim

on-the-wane, children grown and gone.
Who, voice-trained from birth in desire,
wakes one morning wanting—nothing—
in the way of things. Wanting some not-thing
not quite not-seen. Her dreams
—Macy's-parade-balloon-sized dreams—
now lie, a tangle of downed silk and line.
Waist-deep in bright ruin, she labors to sing,
wondering if wanting is, after all, all
there is. Somewhere far away old ice recedes;
somewhere new wars combust. Here, rain is rare
and Pilgrim sings her scales to the dust.
House of no children, guest room of no guest;
no god or guide, a broken song. Her quest.

Why *Pilgrim*?

Yes, *Pilgrim*'s a buzz-kill: dour, dry, dull;
what's cool now is hurling the word,
an insult, at white racists.
Yes, colonists were colonialists
and for Native Americans, *Pilgrim*
means genocide. But weren't some of them
—Anne Bradstreet for one—also idealists,
striving and brave? Look how the word
constellates a whole world: *girl, glim, imp,*
grip, grim, rip, lip, not to mention
the wondrous *pi.* Also, yes, *pig.*
Pilgrim holds—good and bad—what I am,
featured here in its radicle form:
seeker, someone who leaves her home.

Cocktail Party

Cowed by all those straight white teeth,
Pilgrim ran for the bathroom, not for coke
as others supposed, but for something
more covert and rare: a book,
or any bit of anything written. An antidote
to the twitter Out There: the *Times*
or a *Wall Street Journal* stowed by the toilet,
the labels on the bottles of balms
ranked at the sink. She spent one dismal fete
with an issue of *Your Bird Dog Today*—
that taught her the value of purse-cubic-feet
and to bring her own stash—and in this way
she read ninety-nine *Cantos*, near tears
when she thanked her hostess, "Best party in years!"

The Seven Deadly Sins Overheard at the Party

1. GREED, Exercising Noblesse Oblige

"Yes, our house is the size of the *Queen Mary 2*,
but that's okay because we give so much
money away. We made 'Grizzly Patch'
in last year's Bear Hugs Campaign, and guess who
got named 'Redwoods' in the Spring Garden Tour,
and in 41-point font in the program?
No fools we, giving to the private schools
that (and he worked for it, too) will ensure
Billy's admission to Harvard. Thus do loaves
and fishes, tossed on the waters, return
as blue whales to be harpooned again.
The price tag on my suit? What absolves that
is my tailor, whose job depends on this tux:
Brioni, bespoke, and better than sex."

2. PRIDE, Bickering with VANITY

"No, I don't think I'm better than you
because I'm wearing these Birkenstocks
made from recycled rubber. I *like*
how clogs look and don't object to a shoe
made from a near-extinct lizard, flayed
while still alive. And the fourth-grade class tour
of that chicken-farm-cum-abattoir
is not why I'm vegan; no, my birdseed-
and-twigs look *good* next to what you're not
eating." Nearby, Pilgrim, struck by the thought
that not all get to choose portion control,
or can afford organic food, thinks how elite
it all is. Then thinks again: *wait*
—isn't it also elite—just—to eat?

3. ENVY, Envying the Venial Sins

"I don't begrudge your kid landing Harvard,
no. No, in fact, we are really quite pleased
with Gonzales U. And it isn't *schadenfreude*
that accounts for the slow wake of joy
that crosses my face right after you say
your dot.com's gone bust. It's just—
[time   delay   ]—that last dose of Botox
was whale-size, and now I can't smile or frown
on cue. And it's not that I didn't get
your smooth skin, long shiny hair,
expensive shoes, and short skirts I can't wear
because of these varicose veins. What burns
me? The way *some* sins get to be—just—fun,
sins-lite, like a mere toe dipped in brimstone."

4. Lust, Retrieving Her Car

"Yo, Deadly, this ride's hella hot!" He's cute
driving her Bentley, the trim, fit parking valet
now holding the door. Lust likes the hairnet,
and pants riding low beneath the blue jacket
that keeps everything nice and official. When
they talk what's going down later, his plan
"to gangbang all night" makes her cheeks sting
until he explains it's just some street thing
that sounds kind of fun. She wonders where
Mr. Lust is this time—Vegas?—poor dear
left in such a rush, he forgot his cell.
When she picked up, the voice told her to "call
for a good time." Just a butt dial, she's sure.
What pimp would dare phone a husband here?

5. WRATH, Talking about "The Change"

"Menopause is a bitch and, trust me, not
one in heat. Black cohosh and primrose,
soy, and those compounded creams
you rub on your belly. Yuck, and none of it
works—I still hot-flash like a neon sign
in a full *grand mal* fit, I still rail
at water for being too hot. Or cool.
Inappropriate rage? I think not. Mine
is a most perfectly appropriate rage.
What's more fit than fury at heat
and light you must watch while they wane?
We bloom and bloom into old age,
then fade and linger; it's hard not to hate
those new buds that keep swelling the vine."

6. GLUTTONY, Having an Antiphony

"I grow bored with all this fuss about food;
it just leads to digestion and dishes.
The hunger pangs are hot and delicious
and remind me of joy, joy blurred
by memory. I wax in my wane, redeem
the hours I once spent eating meals
made chiefly of lies and a great deal
of washing up. Now there's more time
to savor what matters. In my famine
landscape, each rag and bit of color
is carnival. From the dolor
of hours stung numb, a sermon
of grace is sung. But a tongue never tires
of honey left wild to steep in the comb."

7. SLOTH, Just Wanting to Go for a Sail

"You could say I sonneteer like some sail:
on weekends, in fair weather, ever inside
the curve of a warm, shallow bay. If born
a boat, I'd be that sunfish, tied
in its slip. Or the kayak that unfurled
a parasol for its red sail. Sure, I could
outrace the fleet when in front of the wind,
but tacking? Tedious, too technical.
My sestets and octets—prolapsed. My sail
—slack. But *what is wrong with simply being,*
I think, *in irons*? Why not drop the sheet,
lie back, and bask—ah—in sunset's last heat?
Twilight's pied beauty. An ebb tide rocking the hull.
An eddy. The cry of a lone osprey and gull."

The Ones Pilgrim Likes Best

The ones she likes best? Those who have
suffered the way anyone can suffer:
kids lost to cancer, cults, or drugs; dumped
for younger or richer. The ones not offered
the A-list e-vite—a bummer when a guest
gets too drunk and sobs into the buffet—
but it happens, and then, of course, they
don't come again. Lord, how it shines:
the teeth, the pearls, the chefs in white toques,
the blue-smocked valets, the limestone walks
to houses glowing like over-lit cruise boats
docked under old oaks. Guest cottages
where penitent husbands sleep without fear
that when they weep, the children might hear.

Indentured

after a line by Emily Dickinson

Pilgrim's own teeth, like her parents', are soft
as chalk and will not bleach quite white.
She recalls how her father used to swoop
into the room, *vanting to suck* her blood,
his bridge boiling Polident blue in a cup
on the sink, and her mother making kids
brush twice a day; fluoride fortified not
that tap water, runoff from the mine,
and floss got reused, rinsed, and pinned
to the clothesline. Her father died, if un-
dignified, at least not without art
(the denture case placed over his given-out heart).
Pilgrim's teeth thus far: still in her jaw, and whole.
The better, my dear, to nibble your soul.

The Prime Mover

In Pilgrim's childhood home, the prime mover
was not having enough to pay the bills.
Her father smelled like failure because
he could not pay the bills. At family meals
her mother said they lost the house he'd framed
and she'd laid the floors in, because they couldn't
pay the bills. After the divorce, Dad died
in IRS hock; Mom's heir was Goodwill.
From the *Sears Wish Book,* Pilgrim longed less
for the Things than the glossy intact lives holding
the Things. Weekends, she worked a rag over
a rich family's silver, vowing like Scarlet never
to eat dirt again. So clear then, the rules:
better yourself. Work hard. Save. Pay the bills.

Party Etiquette

1. Remain Upbeat and Polite

Everything was plu-perfect, gosh-darn-it,
till Pilgrim's kid got tagged autistic
and the PTA moms froze her out
with their Tupperware optimistic
"Best for him, too" not to raise hope
re: invites to parties, and Jeez-O-Pete
but when their kids played crack-the-whip
with him the one cracked, into the wall,
it got tough to stay all nice and polite
when they said, "Just a little blood,
boys being boys." Yes, Pilgrim was pissed,
her son razzed every day, maybe twice:
"Got Ritalin?" And about what brick does,
on contact, to a child's perfect face.

2. Elocution

The Swede to her left leaned in
to discuss Pilgrim's "asparagus" son,
worried, it seemed, that his own son
might be part green vegetable too.
Well, it was really the wife who
was worried. *Asparagus, Asperger's,
tomayto, tomahto*—there but for
a few transposed inflections go we—
at Pilgrim's PTA-pep-talk-turned-rant,
a hand had shot up, one baffled mom
frankly stumped. "What's wrong,"
she asked, "with a kid being *artistic*?"
Funny, one letter making a difference,
and just one gene, in an infinite sequence.

3. Don't Talk About This

Tell me, how many times have you
knocked at the locked door
of your son-in-the-bathroom,
wondering if you should this time
kick it in—strobe / flash / of / him / hung
from the shower rod by the belt
of the terrycloth bathrobe you gave him
last Christmas—spring blasted forever,
nuclear winter—and where to find
the manual that tells how to respond
to the loved child who from his snug bed
whispers, *I wish I were dead, Mom*?
Tell me, Dr. Spock, what to do about that,
what does a mother fucking do about that?

Another Party, Another Bathroom

Yes, Pilgrim's at it again, hiding out
with a book while the bright party sparkles
elsewhere. But, throwing the bolt, she sparkles
too, thinking, *This, this is freedom.* She's lit
from within by Augustine: "To Carthage I came
where there sang all around me in my ears
a cauldron of unholy loves." Why, she hears
and can name that tune now! She'd be shamed
if found, B-listed at least, called a kook;
still, she takes the time to touch each towel,
(Frette), the bidet (French), the wallpaper (toile),
the tub-surround tile work. Flips through her book
to her favorite phrase: "take up and read." More,
God, she wants more. Someone bangs at the door.

Archimedes' Lever

Someone bangs at the door, but this time more
loudly: *Hurry up!* Well, he can just piss
off, find another of the six bathrooms this
marble pile affords. Pilgrim's on the floor
eye-to-eye with relic tesserae, the best bit
of mosaic seen since she left Pompeii,
slipping the guard her Gitanes to look away
while she pocketed two tooth-size tiles. It—
this floor—artfully fuses ancient with new.
Think Aristophanes in the mouth of Camus
and Sartre: old ideas, modern milieu.
The tiles are set in cement, but we've seen what a few
cigarettes or million bucks can shake loose.
Her dental tool is titanium. And it fits in her purse.

The News du Jour

Someone's still knocking. It's Ira, a man
outré'd by outrage. "What's your deal?" he grates,
pushing past. "Just take a look at this line."
He's right; they *all* want in. Pilgrim waits,
re-reading a page before flipping him off,
then returns to the party. It's still there.
She wants someone to talk to. Enough
of the holier-than-thou crap, now where
was that Beat Poet they said was a guest?
A bit short in the toothsome department,
but he'd published six books. Duly impressed,
she scans the room. There he is, refulgent
among fans, deploring the news du jour:
genetics, *Real Housewives*, the market, and war.

(The New) Eugenics

They were talking about the new God gene,
saying Spirulina + Divine pills
could not be far behind—take one with meals
to channel Augustine, and to know how
to vote. Others had, if less tolerance,
more hope: "At least we don't rant on late-night TV
for a God who tends only straight white sheep,
and damns the raped strays." All agreed global chants
had not worked, nor mushrooms; tantric sex
was fun. But this gene, in the right hands,
(how hard can it be to sequence two strands?)
could make Manson Gandhi! Stage a Beatles reprise!
Pilgrim felt grim: *Just make sure you spell Lennon*
with an "o" and two "n's"—no more purges, please.

Real Housewives

1. *Stepford Wives* Theme Party

In a parody of a parody inside a parody,
we played charades. This was after hors d'oeuvres:
saltines looped with Cheese Whiz, deviled eggs,
and Campbell's Shrimp Soup dip. We poured
scotch-on-the-rocks, snuck a smoke, and popped
stovetop Jiffy Pop, its swollen tin orb as frail
as a paper wasp nest or spacesuit worn
on the doomed Apollo. Funny at first,
the film featured full skirts topped in chiffon
sheer over bras built by an engineer
who also built rockets nearly as easy to wear.
Watching the wind lash the house on the screen,
we each thought the same thought: *I'm not that girl.*
But when the door blew open, we all felt the chill.

2. Hard to Entertain

It's not easy being a good hostess
to all Seven Sins en masse.
It wasn't always like this. No. I mean, yes,
there were years when every month
brought fledged skies, shy violets and barn owls,
the West Coast a dark, unknown continent.
Then the Sins began to reveal themselves:
her father's strict pact with *ressentiment*,
her mother's wrath, transubstantient
with Percocet. Percocet, chocolate, and gin.
Each morning's ambush, each slept-into noon.
The wish to be anywhere, with anyone
else. The pride masquerading as mean.
The hunger, always through-the-fuse green.

The Market

1. GREED Explains Float

OK, so Dow Jones jumps without
a parachute from Wall Street's corporate jet,
and we're marooned here now, left
giving last rites to a market bereft
of its *Spiritus Mundi.* The plan was
to get-rich-quick-and-get-out, and I still can't
believe it did not trickle down, even one drop.
Or that all the options and futures would not,
like the universe, keep expanding *pi* more years,
or the banks fade so fast, the dollar-bill whores
dialing the Feds before bolting the doors.
They've called all the bets on the bets. Listen—
the whole-world balloon is about to deflate
—and those aren't only mortgages hissing.

2. Clogs for Adidas

The Marin Man is manly, no doubt
about that. He works and plays hard;
he likes womanly women.
Right. Marin Man. Manly. *Fit*
does not begin to describe it.
This guy can run, bike, hike Mt. Tam
and swim the frigid bay,
all in a day's triathlon. And when
he's at ease? Mr. Dad, three shiny kids
and two bird dogs in tow.
He and his kind trade futures no one else
can divine. Lately, he's traded
his clogs for a new pair of Adidas—
traction against those pesky subpoenas.

War

Firouzeh tries to explain her fear
on seeing any partisan slogan,
and how one night, small-son-in-car,
she'd thought they might be
being tailed. She's used to biting her tongue
when Americans presume to blame
her and her kin for the regime
that keeps them gagged and veiled. She begins
with the seeping wound of collective fear
and the issues with travel by air.
When they look confused, she tries again.
"Inmates outnumbered the guards at Dachau,
no? But the guards had the dogs and the guns.
The guards had the guns."

Pilgrim Goes on Retreat

1. Live in the Moment

After three breaths Pilgrim loses track
and has to start over, annoyed at how long
all this is taking. She vibrates, gnashes her teeth.
Gnaws her paw. Watches the clock
like an ADD kid, each   tick   like   eight
years long. The yogini drones on and on
about softening her gut, the last body part
that ever needs urging this way.
Since she's paid twelve bucks for it, though,
Pilgrim tries. *Breathe through your back to open
your heart.* Best, perhaps, not to insist on
being too literal. Best to go with the flow.
Be one, for once, with the blissed-out rest;
yes, this moment's lifer, not its peeved guest.

2. Back from Retreat

Back now from your silent fasting retreat
you no longer feel inappropriate rage
when your cat misses the litter box, nor
do you long to eat her kibble. You can look
directly at your neighbor's full well
without cursing the dowser who charged
half a mil to drill your dry hole.
It's been hard to renounce the Things,
let alone all earthly desire,
but you cope, hoping against hope to save
at least the shoes from the box for Goodwill.
The plan for today: chillax, have a bath.
Do corpse pose. Indulge in the one sin
that brain-dead retreat might condone.

She Learns to Control Her Mouth

1. Situation

Her mouth goes on opening and closing,
and sounds come out: *"Hello!* How've you been,
oh it's been *ages,* yes the high school
applications are *such* a grind . . . "
She tries to focus, nod in the right spots,
keep her smile canyon-wide and not blurt what
she's really thinking: *What? Have you gone out
of your mind? What is that   that   that   that   that
pucker, that sphincter, on your right temple?*
Sure, the rest of the face is smooth and taut,
but this   thing   is a cauliflower, the knot,
she's guessing, where the doc cut the catgut.
And there, Pilgrim reflects, *but for God's grace,
go I. And might go soon—just look at this face.*

2. Resolve

Sometimes they eluded her tutelage
and came spewing out: snakes, lizards, toads,
words that spoke themselves. Like "Cotswold Cottage
my ass, how *ersatz*!" That time, thank God,
her hostess assumed she was praising the cheese
and merely asked, wouldn't Pilgrim
like, also, a bite of the Brie? It was worse
on the days her friends went to see
their plastic surgeons. "It looks like tube socks
stuffed with ping-pong balls!" she would blurt,
"Can't you *see* it?" No. Not at all,
it seemed, no, not at all. Sometimes it hurt,
the endless re-swallowing of reptilian bile,
but she mastered the art of it. For a while.

Oops

Even if those shoes—sorry, those Manolo
stilettos—did cost twice the ticket
for this charity ball, still, Pilgrim gets it:
it was in bad taste to say so,
and to say it so loudly, in that shard
of silence after the nondenominational grace
had *amen*'d. Her bad for getting shitfaced
on the Veuve, and then deciding it would
be funny to swallow that uncut diamond
shaken from its velveteen pouch
and passed from hand to hand to hand,
'round the table. It just went south
from there. Thinking, meanwhile, about Darfur
and *God, all that food.* And the mines so near.

Party On

It was Pilgrim's secret obsession.
Her private, pet bête-noire,
the fear of falling
in love with it all. So she made snide
remarks in her notebook. And went
rather dead inside. But it was hard
to stay depressed at the center
of all that relentless good weather, whether
she liked it or not. So she came back
to life, turned
wholly Deadly instead, resigned
to eventual reassignment
to a place hotter even than L.A. or Vegas.
Yes. She found herself determined to burn.

THE FIRE IS FALLING

You-Know-Where Again

Here she sits again, the door dead-bolted
against the bright party. At last, alone,
free to sneak a smoke and a few lines
from the book shoved into her purse en route.
No one knows I'm here, Pilgrim's first thought
—and in the end her best thought—
followed by the less pleasant doubt
that she'd be very much missed
in the tall Tudor manor tonight where
the Veuve Cliquot brims and the lamb's
trimmed into chops the size of her thumbs.
A martyr sometimes gets hungry and scared,
is troubled by visions, or numbed by scars.
Tonight—all four—as words blur into stars.

Je Est un Autre

after Rimbaud

At that night's party, it happens. You meet
someone you like, very much. True, your new
friend's tastes are a tad parvenu,
and she wears too much bling (take off
the last piece you put on, Mom always said,
to look well bred). Still, you talk books,
politics, not just little Cromwell's score
on the PSAT. What a relief not to be
all alone, how wonderful to agree
on so many things! When you raise a hand
to your hair, though, they catch the light:
your own rings. Yes, it's a mirror, and—shit—
you talking into it. A zero-sum game,
and there you are, inside the gilt frame.

Three-Car Garage

Flaunting your wealth is in poor taste,
Pilgrim tells her kids. And the natives get
envious. That's why Fifth Avenue designed
the "subway coat," discreet black wool lined
with pure mink, farm-raised now, not
like the old days. The Escalade is a sin,
very bad. Pilgrim knows it, but how else
to get all those kids to their match?
Trying her best to mop up the mess
of carbon footprints, she buys gas
that's unleaded and coasts downhill.
Solar-heats the pool. Unplugs the deus
ex machina at night. With friends,
the sedan. Alone, it's the Prius.

Death by Dodge Sportsman

Man Gets Six Years for Motor Home Chase
    —Marin Independent Journal headline

He planned to end it all by "blue suicide"
he said, after the wild, three-hour chase
through the mean streets of Marin and both ways
across the Richmond Bridge. What made
this hot-pursuit sequence unique was not
the peloton of cop cars that trailed him
and could not catch up, but what
he drove to elude them: a motor home.
The twenty-foot '78 Dodge Sportsman
elbowed the sidewalks of each tiny town,
blew red lights, and plowed through more than one
school zone. When he finally stood down,
twelve men with drawn guns forced him to his knees.
Where he waited, whispering, *Please. Just do it. Please.*

Gone to the Dogs

1. We Dogs

We dogs have it pretty good around here.
No leash law, for starters; we run free
in these parts. There's a huge town green
with poop bags on posts. Not that I care,
but *She* sure seems to. Here, Mt. Tam
compounds and distills the exotic smells
of wildcat spoor steamed on noon trails,
and the creeks leap with salmon in spawn.
Our owners L-O-V-E to walk us
or have us walked—all the same to me—
and I like the cultural diversity
from Yorkie to pit bull, with a surplus,
and I do mean surplus, of bird dog thrown in.
God knows why. That dog don't hunt in Marin.

2. You Well May Arf

Some have, shall we say, more than enough,
viz, that pompadoured poodle *française*
chauffeured in her very own chaise
ball-hitched to a bike. *WTF?*
you well may arf, but wait: my friend Prince
the Great Dane gets Rolfed once a week,
and a Shih Tzu I know, an herbal shampoo.
Even *I* got to visit the Dog Whisperer once
to discuss my sometimes-can't-wait need
to—you know—inside. He had this absurd
idée fixe (the crate at night, indeed)
but in the end, he agreed I was right.
Now, life's good. I get great treats, grass-fed beef.
Then, someone brushes my teeth.

Troth

The wicks of his open eyes sunk in paraffin,
my dog's nearly gone. Shaved like a whore,
stapled and stitched and IV-cathetered,
he lies on his side, his monitor beeping
with the same exhausted insistence
as the terrier barking from less-critical-care
in the room beyond. What does *loyal* mean
here? When I was sick or just couldn't sleep,
he stayed up with me. For twelve years,
I knew I'd be missed
if I left, and washed with wet joy
each time I came home.
I'm on my knees, now, leaning in. He turns
his head, smells it's me. He tastes my face.

Refractory

They call it being in shock, this state:
seeing and hearing and breathing but
unable to twitch even an eyelid
at a pinprick or sound of His Master's Voice.
But gasping is not breathing. Snorting
is not breathing. Moaning is not breathing.
Gurgling is not breathing. *Agonal breath,*
the vet said, *before apnea and death;*
the lungs still will bellow after the heart
ceases to beat. She'd heard it before:
less than ten seconds to say yes
to CPR that, with its rubber hose,
would be hard to see, not an E-Z pass.
Pilgrim's father died—twice—like this.

The Truth

I'm ready to tell the truth about Dad,
extolled as a death camp liberator.
He was drunk when he tripped on the stair.
What punctured his lung was his own rib
snapped in three places, not the long blade,
oiled, hung over his tools. He was just a kid,
scared, homesick, hoping not to get killed.
Maybe he did save that Dachau Jew's life
—the letters say so—but he made a pearl
of that memory. Onion skin, sent from Israel,
folded, refolded in the same locked drawer
that held *Ich liebe dichs* from Else, the first girl
my father betrayed. He was false and flawed and still
someone's god, each 3-a.m. sobbed drunk-dial call.

Family Grammar

1. Diction

Oh what's the use in tinkering, dialing
in each word, *memory* for *desire*
so the reader can share the feeling
without feeling lectured? Does the fire
care what phrase names its fierce thirst
or on which beat I break the line?
What metaphor can loosen the vise
closing the actual throat—not just mine,
but hers from an actual tumor—
Mom's face under her sad, festive turban
while she chose the clothes and shoes
to wear for her cremation? There's no use
here for words, the vaunted largesse
of English, or any language. Not for this.

2. Point of View

Well, what the hell else *is* there to do
besides sling words like arrows back
into Fortune's outrageous face? If there's
an alternative palliative, please
tell me now. *The eyes see.* My mother's agon,
each time I raise my voice to my child.
What the hand did. In order to parse
the sentence of the family romance,
diagram it, then repeat it verbatim;
it will not mind being told in a different voice
or from variant points of view:
I, you, he, she, it, we or they
did it to me, you, him, her, us, or them,
or had it done. And so continue to do.

California Dreaming

Corpse pose the yogi said, so I shaped the dead
I'd seen: Mom-and-Dad in the years before
they each died. Light fell short of that notch
in the mountains we called home. I wanted
to stay but could not bear those long, dark days,
so I went west. I went west, lit, and loaded
with cord-stack: the family tree felled by blood,
smoke, and gin. In that first year of dead
and no weather, I wanted winter, trees
with no leaves, any word spoken in tongues.
Stand, he said, *on your head,* and it began to rain.
I dreamt blurred redbud. Outside, upside down,
a tree bled. Like in our backyard at home,
petals—small cups of hope—were blown.

Despair

There's one Deadly Sin not at the party tonight,
and we're her heirs. Don't blame me
that no Canterbury tale or papal decree
saw fit to grant her star billing; this, despite
her being SLOTH's BFF and FAITH's worst foe.
She's the slough all sin spawns in,
the one who was coached to rank linen
by thread count and children by GPA.
She's the one who starved herself gaunt
as Gauguin's *Le Christ jaune* and who woke
one noon to find herself wholly alone.
She'd have said she was happy, if you asked.
(You didn't ask.) The cop sips his Starbucks.
The grapple hook drags Phoenix Lake.

The Bridge

1. Romance

after Eric Steele's documentary film

Panoramic arc and span. One wreck of black
tree. The sea, the sea.
Contrast of verdure and azure. Mica and rust;
dust on the lens and
welts of water like lucent pearls. Fog, a veil
worn to wed your dark love
in a fairy tale. The bereaved, believed to be
sorry now, the friend
who-doth-protest-too-much; not me, please,
please. The inexorable draw of rail.
The struggle, the straddle,
the letting go. The slow
backbend arc of the last on-film fall. A splash,
soft, and off-camera. Silence. Silence and ash.

2. Anastrophe Elegy

Not the woman we all knew. No.
Never would have done she, like this a thing.
How could someone, her, like that ever do?
Knew we the girl: hurdler varsity,
date cute. Sport good. Track quit who
then school to pay rent; for endless hours
tutor of physics; to his M.D,
M.R.S., de Young docent, mother,
cub scout master mistress of,
bleacher-sitter, coach. *The Giver*,
unabridged version of. Middle-aged sprinter,
than ever faster. Lover, a lesion seeping like
after he left her. Empty was found there.
It, at the bridge ramp, still running. The car.

Bane Laid on Behalf of the Latest Late Wife

Let three times in ten years be the charm,
this third suicide no aging trophy wife,
more an it-could-be-you-or-me kind of wife
who got lost in sorrow and shame,
her niece hit-and-run-from on the same day
the divorce decree came in the mail.
I want to say night draped its violet shawl
across the grass where she lay, but she lay naked,
sprawled. Gin, and a fistful of pills to maim
—was it the little-p or big-P?—pain.
All we know is, it's happened again. And again
in our postcard town. Let three times be the charm
that lifts the bane. Or lays it on the men:
may *you* be left. Poison yourselves. Jump. Drown.

Meanwhile, Elsewhere

1. Courtesy Flush

A boy whose name I cannot now recall
in the john with his MK48
did not come out. In e-mails Boy's mom
sent on to the Pentagon: *They made me stand*
on a kid until he bled out. Boy got
his hot-and-cot foursquare meal, time off,
and a week's worth of Paxil. Then returned
to his watch to watch his spirit leach
into the hot sand. *Death by water,* Boy thought,
instead of this slow seep, so he opened
his pump. Zip him in his body bag; toss in
his scarred wrists and the long, long list
of the other un-nameds; God forbid we see
that shit—we'd have to admit it exists.

2. Teleology

In the seed lies all that it can ever be,
shoot, plant, flower, fruit,
and in the end again, the seed.
In the acorn, the entire tree.
A quark encrypts a universe,
a world unfurls from just one joule
of fire. An atom splits and spews
Japan. Blood, bone, gene, and cell
predict events as well as tell them,
and no science, god, or creed
can unwind the strands that bind
our eyes and blind our hands; we walk
a land that's charted. Even as a war
somewhere ends, another war has started.

How Then Shall We Live?

1. The Options

Escape with serial sex
or exercise, a lot.
Join, while you can, the Cult
of the Child. Get lit
on drugs or booze or religion
(for West Coasters, Eastern).
Play the house-trading-up game:
decorate, renovate, redecorate,
roll again. Volunteer to bake,
or bend flower stems
in a glass bowl. Join a cabal
that hikes, or reads the classics.
Divorce. Kill yourself
in a way that leaves the least mess.

2. Couldn't She Just

after a line by Sylvia Plath

The options, so far, not good. Suicide?
No, perfection may not have children,
but she has three. Divorce?
No, she still loves her husband. Divest
her spousal share? See divorce, ibid.
But, could it be less all-or-none
than she'd assumed? Might not small acts
accumulate? Couldn't she just—downsize?
—give stuff away? Grow something,
read more, watch less TV?
Remind herself there are other zip codes?
Love her family in situ and not
how she'd planned they would be?
—couldn't she just—love her family?

Syringes "R" Us

Underneath all that irony and wit
lurked something not all that funny,
something sort of sad. Like that sign
she'd seen in the Tenderloin,
Syringes "R" Us. A real gut-buster
at first. And then. And then. And then not.
Lately it was more often not
than not, and she felt blindsided. Bleak.
Hormonal. In a bad mood. Oh shit,
just say it, Pilgrim was S-A-D sad.
Prozac helped until she got numb
to being numb all the time, and the pain
came back. *Ashes, ashes, we all fall down.*
Same old plague. New superbug strain.

Ennui

It hit her like a double bolus of morphine.
Her problem was ennui. Envy of ENVY.
Pilgrim wished she could, but just did not care.
Not about shoes, blow-dried hairdos,
ins to swank parties, flat stomachs and house lots,
toddlers locked and loaded on Harvard,
sugar in schools, or Land Rovers v. Escalades.
(OK, maybe a little about the shoes.) She lacked
a certain *je ne sais quoi*, but for, well,
any *quoi* at all. And wasn't that its own sin?
To have it all, and still be malign and vile,
a wart on the face of esprit de corps?
Perhaps she needed to dial it back:
booze and Prozac. Recall pain for a while.

On the Wagon

Curse you, brown bottle beaded with dew,
your long cool draught on a hot July day
and damp-newsprint-page night; I detest
your fresh-bread taste, your cold heft
in my hand. Curse you, thick mug of dark rum,
warm in the cold nights and mornings come,
too soon, after; I hate how you burn down
my throat, turn liquid the ice of my bones.
Curse you, red wine in a thin crystal globe,
viscous and luscious and round as the world,
how you draw blood to my lips, force-bloom
my March mouth, gold-leaf a gray room.
Your slug of raw silk and smoke, its hot lick
at the back of my throat—thick, thick with ache—

Bourbon Elegy

I miss your tongue
on my spine

the crack of your fist
on my jaw

the pleasure of pain
going numb

the pitch and yaw
when my brain

clicked and changed
channels

the everythingbeautifulblur
jagged pink smear

of each cracked-windowpane
shade-undrawn dawn

Religion

Even today is my complaint bitter. . . .
Oh, that I knew where I might find Him!
                    —Job 23:2-3

Pilgrim knew what the answer was: get born
again. Even if it hadn't worked out
so well the first time. The altar-call part,
the prophesying, the speaking-in-tongues
all felt a lot like a Ouija board cheat,
you know, wanting it so much that, OK,
SHE NUDGED THE PLANCHETTE. And if it
spelled, before they met, her first love's name?
She doubted it all the same, having been,
as it were, that portent's chief engineer.
She found the kill switch (every miracle has one)
to pop, pre-inflation, each birthday balloon.
In this way she outwitted salvation
and could keep both kitten heels on the ground.

the fire is falling

a september wedding back at the cape—
three days without kids—then he'll work
in new york while she flies back
to san francisco alone—a good plan
till she misses her plane—she's en route
to boston when the fire is falling
and he's in midtown—the circuits jammed
and she's holding hands with a stranger
in the qwik-stop—then sitting on the curb
for a long time—for a long time dialing—
the fire still falling when he picks up—
the plume somewhere behind him—the fire
falling—as it always has—this close—
it has to be this close before she sees

Nuns Fret Not

after Wordsworth

Pilgrim's inside the frame here and guesses
she's liked it that way. If nuns fret not
in their narrow cells, why then should she?
Her cot has, after all, got this very nice mattress
and custom duvet. But under the green hum
of the all-night lights she—almost—makes out
some other sound. A break in the rhythm,
a knock in the engine of warm rocking dark
(for the lights in their way do emit darkness)
—the men on their knees in the dirt
of the park she jogs in, a Food Not Bombs T-shirt,
a friend's son's legs lost in Iraq—Iraq?
What is Iraq doing in here? She's screwed.
Something *is* knocking. The size of a world.

O EARTH RETURN

Prayer for My New Daughter

A soul in chrysalis, in first agonized molt,
must choose: LADIES or MENS.
For some—for you—these rooms are fraught,
an open field where lines are drawn: think of
the White-Only signs. Or Serrano's *Piss Christ*
and Duchamp's *Fountain*, pitted with acid
and icepicks, de-faced. As for restrooms called
"Bathrooms with Urinals," no, his words
will never deconstruct the master's house.
For an hour I have walked and prayed,
considering icepicks, how they're made
to fit a blind hand; how kept so well honed.
You are soft as sown grass and fierce as cut glass.
You pack your new purse with lipstick, and mace.

The Master's House

Take me, says this long, languid lick
of limestone and slate-roof house

corseted by a whalebone-thin fence
anyone could unlace

or shinny over onto the lush lawn.
Inside, the living room light

(curtains left loose and undrawn)
precisely at dusk, clicks on.

At the gate, ten bundles of newsprint
lie where thrown,

their lips peeping from plastic
and swollen with rain.

All of it whispering—*go ahead*—*go*—
no one's at home to say no.

Rat Diptych

1. Secondary Poison

"Only the *best* places have rats." This from
the realtor when Pilgrim called to complain,
and, "Haven't you been to Bouchon?
Their rats are bigger than your bichon frise,
and look out, or they'll carry him off!"
It wasn't that much of a comfort, but
she learned to bait with d-CON, and cough
before binning the trash. She found it—
the pack-rat midden—behind the shed door,
getting whipped by a nude tail (*quelle horreur!*)
in the set-to that ensued. How much more,
she couldn't not think, could a person endure;
how bad could it get? She found out, when her
cat ate the rat that ate the d-CON that . . .

2. Extreme Rendition

The rodent technician's recommendation:
a "Havahart" trap, kinder than the clamp
with triangle teeth or the spring-bar garrote.
She was down with the plan: illegal dumping
—her shit into someone else's yard—but what
if the rat found its way back? And was pissed?
Was part of a cell with widespread connections?
Wood rats are native (and cute), but sometimes
it can be difficult to tell a wood rat
from a rat who would like to kill you.
Problem: dead's not an option here in Marin.
Fix: relocate, with upgrade, to a place
where a rat can be loved. And, with excess.
Orange County, perhaps. Or Crawford, Texas.

Rebuke

What does the loon cry out to the lake
and the lake repeat to the rain?
The birds sing high in the old pine,
while this cabin's wide floorboards
betray us: raw, white as bone,
still sticky with sap. We compost, we sort
our trash that then gets disappeared
to a plant where nothing alive is sown
or grows. Except for the black-dotted-line
of crows, pecking at human alluvium,
paper and plastic massing a mountain
we finally cannot not see. What does the loon
cry out to the lake, the lake repeat to the rain?
What is the meaning of any refrain?

Forgotten Image

after Gaston Bachelard's The Poetics of Space

Your mother, reading, on the stairs in light
poured in a wide shaft. At night, shadows,
soft thuds and pleading, clink-clink of his ice
in the glass. Your mother, reading. Light seen
through a chink in a cellar wall. The attic air,
dry and danced with bright motes. You know
it's there, at the top of the house, the stairs
you must muster the mind to ascend. But how?
Where is the first step? Your old notebooks,
dust-felted, stacked up somewhere. Your mother,
reading. The sense of another life, inside
and outside the walls. An attic, other upper rooms
in the home. Other homes. You are a mother now,
too—so many open mouths, so much to do—
your mother, reading herself alive. Showing you.

Bright Juice

Full fathom five Pilgrim's mother lies
north of the old shuttered silk mill
where each visiting fourth-grade girl
was given a bobbin wound with floss
shiny and fine as a spider's thrown line.
I have mine still, and the memory
of mulberries staining my hands,
the refrain of juice bright in my mouth.
At my mother's wake, other gray faces
who'd worked the looms in rooms
so thick with thread that noon
was dark. *Of her lungs is shantung spun.*
A spider spills herself, shining, in air,
and beauty's matrix is mucous and fear.

Blazon

Azure, a bend Or: sunset against sky.
Party per pale argent and vert: a tree
counterchanged by twilight. *Cyan*:
the sea-flooded dune, tincture of silver,
the sand your hair combed by ebb tide.
A beach rose *gules* for your cheeks, your eyes
mudflats brimming with moon.

The last tide is poised to turn again soon,
and I resign hope to its neap. Then remember
you, daughter, born in a scarlet welter
on a wave's green-curled edge of pain.
Your glad, loud cry, your father's shout,
the great gout of joy when I recognized
your face, new morning's high tide, its blaze.

Food Not Bombs

Daughter, your taper is so slender
and burns so hot in this wind
like a wall of asphalt.
Your hands cup the paper plate
into a skiff to float you away
from the continent of one man's hunger.
Your eyes are flame,
so full of his pain
I cannot bear to look in.

But because of you I must look in.
His eyes are blue, too. He tells us
his name—Tampa—and each call
he heard at dawn in the brush:
Mockingbird. Robin. Chickadee. Thrush.

How to Live, Reprise

The world was not as she'd been taught
laundry one neatly sorts
into blacks and whites;
it is gray with children
and other defenseless acted-upons.
All you can do, Pilgrim decides,
is keep asking the questions.
Admit when you're wrong. Go on
for the kids, especially the kids
you have personally caused
to be brought into the world.
As far as you can, regardless,
clean up your own mess.
Do not use bleach on every load.

I'll Burn My Books

She hadn't always been like this, bitter to bone,
but Pilgrim found for a time she understood
how the delicate soupçon of wormwood
could make every dish tried into one
relished cold. She liked the bite of saltpeter,
that feel in her mouth, the blue feel of steel,
until someone made the metaphor real
and really died. When the family rose to stand for
the last prayer—agony's diorama—
Pilgrim thought, *What if the world IS conclusion?*
And, *What those kids need is a mama
who's breathing.* Bitter began to hurt her again,
scorn burned her tongue. Finding herself long on
words but short of breath, she put down her pen.

Twelve-Step Meeting

The women in these rooms dwell in paradox.
Some train verbal Uzis on each *man, he,* and *his*;
others darn the worn socks of clichéd phrase.
These are the evenings of Just-Shoot-Me-Now,
beginning with a squat, spitting candle
passed hand-to-hand, ending with blown breath
and spent light. Sometimes a song rings out,
sometimes cant, or I-can't-take-any-more;
then one, then the next one, will weep. Tonight,
for Pilgrim, the old-timers stand down.
She rises and waits while they dim the dim lights,
then pulls from her clutch the small, silver knife
she'll wield to lay herself wholly open
from mouth to crotch: one thin red, honest line.

Dirt

"I was the dirt of the dirt," Pilgrim said,
testifying about *How It Was,*
and it hurt her to say it. So much, that
she said it again. *What Happened?*
At the first meeting she could not make out
the words when others were sharing;
it took a year to recall any name
said after her own. *What It's Like Now?*
She repeated her line, feeling hot, stung,
sealed in her hair shirt. Then it hit her
that having a powerful itch to scratch
meant she was alive. As for dirt, *Let Us Pray*
we'll learn to like it. That's all we get: today.

All Dirt Is Holy

From Santa Fe I planned to drive north
through the mountains of Sangre de Cristo,
but my wheel turned itself to wind down
into a green-pinyoned valley: Chimayó.
A church. Inside, cool dark, an altar with icons
and candles, and a back room of raw earth
strewn with *milagros*: crutches, prosthetics,
glass eyes. Father Roca said, *God alone heals,*
not what's back-hoed off-site and trucked in
by night to this room. Still, I drank the dirt tea
of desert, arroyo, sky, and high chaparral,
and what I disbelieved drew me to a well
where I knelt and dug and held in my hands
a world of white birds and linen and wounds.

If Not, Winter

How the night air smells like Circe's island,
like frangipani, even the trees a species
of rose. Grapevines bound in precise chords
tracing contours of hills. Orchards knee-deep
in wild mustard along I-5, forget-me-nots
blue in the ruts. Silver chains of salmon
hauled up mountain streams. Live oak, wild orchid,
purple owl clover. Mt. Tam's cubist nude
in recline, alpenglowed. Persimmons hung
like bright lanterns after the leaves have gone.
Houseboat gypsy scarlets and azuls,
gray gulls, parchment egrets. Frail sculls
pulling diagonals on wide pewter water,
looking back while drawn into the future.

Vernal

Some things we believe cannot be redeemed.
But in a valley the Railroad finally forgot,
the silted, slugged ditch we would not eat fish from
runs again, a river, rilled as before
by clear water, not black. Grass grows back
between tracks and rails. Limestone spalls
hewn from the mountain heal into soil.
Stumps heaped with live coals, split, and winched out,
in spring frail a new circlet of green.
Panthers are seen. A son is born blue, and lives.
Some things we believe cannot be redeemed,
but the dawn, as yet, is diurnal. The woods keep
a hushed vigil, then rustle with life we can't see;
small ponds well from the ground while we sleep.

The Quest

The quest was a metaphor, of course
—it *could* mean abroad in a world
where May keeps blooming
right through one's own fall—but also:
just asking the questions. No longer
not-seeing suffering, not for
the *thank-God-it's-not-me* effect of, more
like bearing witness. Maybe the chance
to do an angstrom of good, make beauty
or protest or laughter. Any act
for those who (despite dire reports, still)
keep coming after. A gimbal stable
in drift, apparent wander. A dance
done with wonder—in every sense.

Contradance

Restore Thine image, so much, by Thy grace,
That Thou mayst know me, and I'll turn my face.
—John Donne

An apostate apostasy called out to me
not to turn away from Love
even if Love turned away from me.

His shadow was long and conjoined with mine,
and so I took my place in the line.

I held my breath, and breath held me

—the moth to the blue-tipped flare,
the raptor's relation to air—

I'll love you forever like you once loved me,

he said, then led me in Gypsy Meltdown.
We walked a wide circle that pinned my eyes to his.
I fell back into the back of a great green wave,

I fell into the swell of a great green wave,
I was the flung shell of the sea.

Preparation for Pirouette

When my newborn lay gray, silent, and still,
I saw a notch in the skin at his collarbone—a petal
puckered by rain or, over an open mouth, a veil
of chiffon sucked in—breath's first pirouette.
When my mother lay dying, what pierced me
was not her mouth's black puckered O. It was not
her hands going slack at the rails, or even her eye
sunk into iris-less stone. It was that last breath
shirring the flesh at her throat, the sign that she
—drawn utterly inwardly taut—was braced
to her clenched core against death. One day, my turn
to make a wreath of my arms, rise up *en pointe*—

        then, whip-pivot-spot—be gone.

Let my throat ache then, be notched. Each flawed dawn.

NOTES

"Why *Pilgrim*?" Part of the Winthrop Fleet of Puritan emigrants in 1630, Anne Dudley Bradstreet was the first woman poet to be published in both England and America. A seeker among seekers, Bradstreet reveals in her poems a somewhat ambivalent pilgrim, in love with the world and struggling to maintain the piety demanded by her faith.

"The Seven Deadly Sins, Overheard at the Party." The pageant of the allegorized Seven Deadly Sins is a familiar trope in literature, appearing in works by St. Paul, Chaucer, Dante, Spenser, Augustine, Aquinas, Blake, Spenser, Marlowe, Goethe, Bunyan, C.S. Lewis, and many others. In descending order of perfidy, the sins are Pride, Avarice (Greed), Envy, Wrath (Anger), Lust, Gluttony, and Sloth (sometimes aligned with Despair).

"SLOTH, Just Wanting to Go for a Sail." "Pied Beauty" is from Gerard Manley Hopkins's curtal sonnet by that name. The references to "prolapsed" octets is from James Fenton's discussion of "Pied Beauty" in *An Introduction to English Poetry* (Farrar, Straus and Giroux, 2002).

"Indentured." The last line is an allusion to these lines from Emily Dickinson's "This World Is not Conclusion:" "Much Gesture, from the Pulpit — / Strong Hallelujahs roll — / Narcotics cannot still the Tooth / That nibbles at the soul—"

"Another Party, Another Bathroom." The quote is from *Confessions*, by St. Augustine of Hippo.

"(The New) Eugenics." God Gene theory hypothesizes a specific gene predisposing some people toward spirituality or mysticism. Dean Hamer, *The God Gene: How Faith Is Hardwired into Our Genes* (Anchor, 2005).

"Hard to Entertain." Not quite the same as resentment, *ressentiment* implies a cautious, defeatist, or cynical attitude and belief that the individual and human institutions exist in a hostile or indifferent universe or society.

"Death by Dodge Sportsman." The headline ran in the *Marin Independent Journal* on 10/9/08.

"Family Grammar," "Point of View." The quoted phrases are after Robert Lowell's line "my eyes have seen what my hand did" in "Dolphin."

"Courtesy Flush." The poem was inspired by a PBS report in 2008 estimating that more than 1,000 U.S. soldiers had taken their own lives during the wars in Afghanistan and Iraq.

"Syringes 'R' Us." The gritty blocks of San Francisco's Tenderloin district still resist gentrification. A superbug is a pathogen that has acquired resistance or immunity to antibiotic treatment.

"the fire is falling." "The fire, the fire is falling!" is from "A Song of Liberty" by William Blake.

"Prayer for My New Daughter." This poem responds to Yeats's "A Prayer for My Daughter," and borrows from his line "And for an hour I have walked and prayed." Icepick lobotomies were considered legitimate "treatments" for gay and transgender people in this country through the 1950s.

"Blazon." The first stanza of this poem is written in the syntax of and using the terminology of heraldry.

"I'll Burn My Books" is from Christopher Marlowe's *The Tragical History of the Life and Death of Doctor Faustus,* and recalls Prospero saying in *The Tempest,* "I'll drown my book."

"Dirt." "O earth return" is after the "Introduction to the Songs of Experience" by William Blake.

"All Dirt Is Holy." Travelers to the chapel in Chimayó, New Mexico, enter a small candlelit room behind the shrine and kneel near the *pozito* (little well) to scoop out *tierra bendita* (sacred earth) to be made into tea or rubbed on the body to cure illness, wounds, or pain. *Milagro* means "miracle," and *milagros* are ex-votos, or votive offerings.

"If Not, Winter" is one of Sappho's fragments and the name of a book of translations of her work by Anne Carson: *If Not, Winter: Fragments of Sappho* (Knopf, 2002).

"Preparation for Pirouette" owes a debt to Leon Stokesbury's poem "Watching My Mother Take Her Last Breath."

A Note from the Author

Thank you to the (many!) readers of this book who gave invaluable feedback during its various incarnations and to Tom Lombardo for choosing the manuscript that finally emerged. I'm grateful to all the journal editors who published these sonnets, but I owe special thanks to editors Paula Deitz of *The Hudson Review*, Orlando Menes of *Notre Dame Review*, and Wayne Chapman of *The South Carolina Review*. My deep appreciation goes to Molly Peacock for her inspired guidance on structure and to Susan Griffin, whose steady support and belief in the work enabled me to keep believing, too.

REBECCA FOUST won the 2015 Press 53 Award for Poetry for *Paradise Drive*. Her other books include *God, Seed: Poetry & Art About the Natural World* (Tebot Bach, 2010), a collaboration with artist Lorna Stevens that received a 2010 Foreword Book of the Year Award; *All That Gorgeous Pitiless Song* (Many Mountains Moving, 2010), which received the 2008 MMM Press Poetry Book Prize; and two chapbooks, *Mom's Canoe* (Texas Review Press, 2009) and *Dark Card* (Texas Review Press, 2008), both winners of the Robert Phillips Poetry Chapbook prize. Foust earned an MFA from Warren Wilson College in 2010 and is the recipient of fellowships from The Frost Place and The MacDowell Colony. She lives and works in the San Francisco Bay Area as a writer, freelance editor, teacher, and Marin Poetry Center board member.

Cover artist Suzanne Engelberg is a fine art photographer based in the San Francisco Bay Area. She is especially interested in interpretive landscape photography. Her work has been exhibited in galleries across the country and she has received  numerous awards, including awards from the New York Center for Photographic Art, Professional Women Photographers, and the Grand Prix de la Couverte. She is the author of *Visions of Phoenix Lake*.

 Cover designer Lorna Stevens is a mixed media artist interested in visually exploring culture and nature. Her work has been acquired by the Brooklyn Museum, the di Rosa, the New York Public Library, the Numakunai Sculpture Garden, and the SF MOMA Research Library. She received her MFA from Columbia University and teaches collage and sculpture at City College of San Francisco.

CPSIA information can be obtained at www.ICGtesting.com
Printed in the USA
LVOW07s2203021015

456787LV00003B/67/P